ASSARACUS

A Journal of Gay Poetry
Issue 2

SiblingRivalryPress

Assaracus
A Journal of Gay Poetry
Issue 2: April 2011
ISBN 978-0-9832931-1-8
ISSN 2159-0478
Bryan Borland, Editor
Copyright © 2011 by Sibling Rivalry Press, LLC

Cover Art, "Fallen Angel" by Michael Moran. Used by Permission. Artist's website is www.angelstudiostore.com.

Sibling Rivalry Press, LLC
13913 Magnolia Glen Drive
Alexander, AR 72002

www.siblingrivalrypress.com

ASSARACUS

WONDER DAVE

you have made us icons

Wonder Dave is a traveling writer and performer from the Midwest now living in northern California. He has garnered multiple awards and accolades for his work including an appearance on group piece finals stage at the National Poetry Slam in 2010 and receiving the Jerome Foundation's Verve Grant in 2007. Dave has been a featured poet throughout the U.S., performing at poetry shows, burlesque revues, book stores, universities, theatre festivals, and even once on the center lanes of a bowling alley. The poem "Crime Scene," included here, was featured in the June 2010 issue of *The Legendary*.

www.wonderdave.net

ALL AROUND THE MULBERRY BUSH

Your stomach is a jack-in-the-box
He grabs you by the hips
your crank turns

an unruly bike ride no hands
You are all around the mulberry bush
monkey, weasel, clown

You listen to the club music it sounds
simple, tinny, repetitive
it is one hour and fifteen minutes

until last call he grabs
your hips that's the way the money goes
tonight you will see no sidewalk sale

you listen to the music
think of children's toys
spread out on a blanket

twenty-five cents a pop
see a plastic red box with a wooden handle
your stomach is churning

you ask him for a ride home
a cab would have cost ten dollars
you feel cheap

He says yes as the song ends
grips the handle
sends you spinning

tonight you think it is all in fun
waiting for the clown
to spring, the music starts again

DELILAH HAS HER SAY

All you remember is that I cut Samson's hair
Even there you are a bit off
I lulled him to sleep and watched it happen
There is more to me than your 16 verses in Judges

Maybe you remember that
the Philistines gave me money to betray him
I took it and ran so far away

I never spoke Hebrew again
whispered that hair
grows back

I was not a Philistine
My name is Hebrew

I was born in the Sorek valley
a part of Gaza
even then it was a war torn country

The valley was the border between
the Philistines and the Israelites
My family had a vineyard there
the battles left flames swishing like fox tails
through our fields

The name Delilah means
one who makes impoverished

My parents named me for the burden
of a baby born in a bad season
with my first breath I tasted burnt earth

You could hardly call me treacherous

Each night I asked him plainly,
"Samson, what is the source of your power?
How can you be bound?"

Each night he joked a little white lie:
7 wet bow strings
newly woven rope
braid cloth into my hair

In the morning he would shrug off the shackles
he had requested the night before
Even the rope of an ox cart snaps like a twig
when the strength of god is in your shoulders

Eventually Samson told me the secret of his hair
how he had been Nazirite since birth
but before that he told me how

with his bare hands he'd ripped the head off a lion
Imagine how your hands would look
He had killed thousands of men
He described in vivid detail how jawbones cut through necks
Imagine how you would look at your hands

I began to notice
the unnatural strain of his back
the bloodstains in the creases of his knuckles
the way his legs twitched constantly
like he had somewhere to run

I decided that no man should have to carry
the wrath of god in his muscles

As I watched the locks be snipped from his head
I saw his shoulders relax
for the first time in his entire life

THINGS I WON'T CARE ABOUT THIS FEBRUARY

Ground hogs
Valentines
My birthday
The absent days at the end of the month

The way street lights illuminate snow
The way cars crash into the median because of the slush
Paying my rent on time
Work slowing down
The subsequent smaller paychecks

The afterglow of sex with you
The house we lived in together
The way three years after our break up
       you have found your way into all my poems at last

SHOTGUN (HEART BREAKER PART 2)

Some of us were built for breaking hearts
unaware of our own construction
the smooth wood of our necks
our hungry bellies

We are gorgeous shotguns
You are the shell
the plastic case empty
scattered buck shot

Don't fancy yourself a target
We don't even know what we're shooting at
We only want to be left smoking
like a silver screen beauty

I've always thought things
looked best after they had been spent
I remember the first time

I caught myself doing it
put on the safety
opened the chamber
took him in knowing
he would be discarded

The comfort of his soft flesh
the way I listened when he shared his dreams
like I was willing to be a part of them

DIRTY DANCING (HEART BREAKER PART 3)

Some of us were built for breaking hearts
or more accurately

Some of us will punch through your sternum
fish around innards
until we find that pulsing fist sized
bastard organ

Then we will proceed to reenact
the end sequence of "Dirty Dancing"
while clutching it firmly

Because I had
the time of my li-i-ife
and I owe it all to yooou-ooh

throwing your emotions
to the floor and
kick ball change,
kick ball change,
kick ball changing
all over them

Blood and tears smeared everywhere
We will leave you unrecognizable
like Jennifer Grey post nose job

In other words
We gon' fuck you up sugar
real bad

Don't step to me with
your innocent smile
and sweet baby cheeks

Please
I have done this dance
more than enough times
leave me alone

VORPAL BUNNIES

We have existed among you since time immemorial
You have made us icons
carved our image into cathedrals
you can still see a knight fleeing
from us Notre Dame

It seems though that in modern times
you have forgotten to fear us
you have turned us into propaganda
put us on the cover of your cereal boxes

You speak cutely of our sexual prowess
dress your women in our ears and tails
You told your children I would bring them candy
I will leave them drained vegetables

Ancient Man have called us
Totochtin and Kalulu
You can call me BUNNICULA
Lord of the Killer Rabbits
My name is shall be mankind's DOOM

Long ago your knights of the square table tried
to vanquish me but I would rise again
to battle President Carter in the swamp
He paddled away in terror before I could sink my
fangs through his neck

You sent your academy award winning actress
Glenn Close to boil me alive

I would not be stopped
I bided my time
Made allegiances with the White Rabbit,
the March Hare, Breer Rabbit,
Babs, Buster, Quik, Gabrielle,
and my super soldiers Flopsy, Mopsy and Cotton Tail

We've spent the last three decades perfecting an army
increasing our numbers
or as you mangy furless bipeds would say
"We fucked liked Bunnies"

I have fathered
quick and clever tricksters
with hind legs strong enough
to thump through your skulls
leave your brains leaking like Cadbury cream

We shall descend upon you
ravage your carrot patches
bring glorious mutant hybrid jackelopes
to gore out your spleens

we will attack by land air and sea
we will bring your Water ships Down

When this army hops over the horizon
you will be overwhelmed by the cuteness
at first

then you will see death in our eyes
realize your shotguns are worthless
even after bodies fill with buck shot
we just keep going and going and going

As our fuzzy brigade of nightmares zig zag toward you
you will wonder how we Rabbits
know so much about where you go to hide
you small eared fools never even noticed
our velveteen spies among you

You will see us coming
ready to scoop you up and bop you on the head
by the time you realize what has befallen you
it will be too late, too late on this very important date

Humanities reign will come to an end
from this day forward it shall always be
the year of the Rabbit

FAT BOY

You were my first fat boy
Yes there were broad shouldered fellows
And husky gentlemen before you
But you were the first one anyone would call FAT

Thick thighs, strong calves
handful breasts with perky pink nipples
If you were a woman we would have called you
pear shaped

you had big ass

Round and you used to shake it on the dance floor
like the whole world was watching and you
didn't give a fuck

I remember your ass
fondly

While we were never boyfriend material
you were the best fuck buddy
I ever had

You were acrobatic in bed
your wide legs spread eagle
belly & butt jiggling with each thrust

the sex was so good
it made that time you gave me crabs
worth it

I hear you're a top now
I find this surprising

Not as surprising
as when you left town
only to come back just over a year later
and a 120 pounds lighter

I told you that you looked great
I didn't know how to say I missed your booty
I couldn't tell you the lean torso
and defined muscles

that had garnered you so much new attention
looked all wrong to me
Maybe had I been there to see the pounds shed away
one week at a time it would have been different

The truth is rooted in cliché
I liked you better when you were bigger
I loved you more when there was more of you to love
You still dance like the whole world is watching
but you don't smile when you do it

I miss the fat boy
I miss the empty space
you are no longer capable of filling

BETTIE PAGE

Bettie Page,
for you I would be
etched onto forearms, biceps and thighs

cast as a tattoo bombshell
dark curls rest like snakes on bare shoulders

We live
in snuff film heaven
winking at the camera

We are cigar smoke
thick and blue; lurking around ankles
banned from bars
you can still smell us in the floor boards

Bettie if your skin is die cast hand painted metal
are you to be collected

They finally made you hard
wished Medusa's curse-gift into reverse

give me that metal skin
make me pant like Jenna Jameson until
I never want to fuck off camera again

Paint me beautiful
I am damaged
with vixen red lips
say that is not the problem

stretch me across canvas
make me understand the power of lust in two dimensions

Bettie I was wondering
will these snake bites on my collar bones ever heal

do you ever get tired of staring at stones

CRIME SCENE

My dating history is not unlike a crime scene.

I present to you the suspects:

1. Just because he's on anti-psychotics doesn't mean he's not fucking crazy.
2. The bar manager with one nut and no ability to be emotionally available.
3. Any man that I have ever crossed paths named with Dan.
4. The boy who left me for Jesus. Twice.
5. Redacted at his request.
6. A drunk.
7. A straight guy.
8. Another drunk.
9. A recovering drunk.

Through the glass of retrospect I stare at this police line up of men, multiple of whom are actually convicted felons, and think where did I go wrong?

Should I have stayed with my high school sweetheart? Is it that 1950's sitcom simple? The last time I was in Milwaukee he bought me a bagel and cranberry juice as we reminisced about a relationship that vanished a decade ago. At the scene of the crime he left a steamed up 89 Bonneville parked by the river. My fingerprints are all over this one in fact they are everywhere mad and primary like a kindergarten finger painting.

1. You are so worthwhile I wish I could prove it to you.
2. Maybe I should not fuck the management and about that time I waited outside your building at four am for you to come home; sorry.
3. Seriously guys named Dan wtf?
4. Your parents did a number on you. I'm glad you're doing better these days.
5. Redacted because he promised to have sex with me again.
6. When you get sober don't call me.
7. Get your tongue out of my mouth you are heterosexual.
8. Full disclosure: The second drunk was only on the first list because I liked the cadence.
9. I can hardly say your name.

At the scene of my crime you will find; a leather bound journal, a purple cowboy hat, a blue comforter and a bottle of scotch, several bottles of scotch. Butterflies and intestines are pinned to the walls with kitchen knives. The air is a funny kind of bitter-sweet like flowers purchased for yourself. If this scent could be captured on film it would look exactly like my mug shot.

MOHRING
RON

all this will be yours

Ron Mohring is the author of the poetry collection, *Survivable World*, which won the 2003 Washington Prize. He lives in central Pennsylvania, where he manages Seven Kitchens Press, publisher of the annual Robin Becker Chapbook Series. Five of these poems have previously published: "Arrival" in *West Branch,* "Following Lorca" in *Carnegie Mellon Poetry Review*, "Hair" in *Phoebe,* "Peg of My Heart" in *Bay Windows*, and "The Sound" in *Bloom*.

sevenkitchenspress.wordpress.com

EITHER, OR

It happens as I'm bent before the oven, my right arm thrust in its hot
lion's mouth, grabbing the bubbling pizza. When I fall
I'll bash my head neatly into the rack. I'll be glad not to feel my hand
sizzle against its baleful tongue. As I climb the stairs, laundry basket
jammed into my paunch, I'll trip on the cat, crash hard to one knee.
The fresh clothes will cascade as I flail and catch myself,
wrenched but intact. I'll bark a laugh, then cough, then choke
as my heart decides to kick me while I'm down.
If it's winter and the sidewalk ice must have me,
I pray that my dog will stay out of the street till I'm found.
If a little pipe bursts in my brain as I turn from the board,
let the book tumble gently from my hand. Let them believe
that in that moment I was utterly theirs. Let the other driver escape
my sudden veer. Allow the crossing night creature its passage intact.
Carry me through the last quarter-mile of my walk,
and send my chatty friend home with fresh-cut dahlias
before I am felled in the garden. Let the earwig
enter my ear. Let me slump into the rain-swollen ditch, bubble
one final word to the waving grass. No, wait. Let me go back.
Let me write sweet notes to my love and slip them into the fat
Selected Neruda. Then let it be quick: passing a rickety scaffold,
a board or brick to the head. Suck me from the plane and let me fly.
Kick me like a stone from the edge of the bridge. Lay me out,
lay me down. Let my love settle happily, in time,
with a man half his age, a bedroom acrobat who nightly
cleans his clock then sleeps curled round him like a cat.
Let them sip champagne from each other's mouths, grow to love figs
and poetry, decide one rainy afternoon to read the Neruda. Look: the pages
fanning slowly open on the bedside table as they grapple and moan.

THE FIRES

Andrea sweeps her white skirts
north into the Atlantic. She's leaving
in a snit, refuses to accommodate
the weather prayers: on the TV
satellite image, a hazy line of smoke
drifts from Florida's blunt
downturned thumb, right into her eye.

This is not California.

Once, driving from college
on a weekend trip to Virginia,
we passed through a ragged fire:
thick smoke obscured the road.
Loud snap of burning trees. A soot-
faced man waved us through.
Fraternity boys, we were useless.

Birds, overcome, fall from the sky.

What would you save if you had
twenty minutes? Five? What makes
you think that all this constitutes
a self? Better to feed
it all to the ravenous flames.
To drift untethered at last.

MEMORY, SIX-SIDED, LIKE A DIE

Miss Kitty sleeps on her back, paws pushing
air. Eddie thrashes, his skin clammy. The sheets
already damp. Rigo gets up for thermometer, towels.
Eddie moans in his sleep.

&

his body had begun to swell, and

&

One car dead in the driveway. The ripped side
filled with two years of leaves. Eddie doesn't want
to think about it: stalemate. If Rigo loved him more
he'd simply have it hauled away. He'd take care of it.

&

WANTED: HOUSEMATE TO SHARE
WITH GAY COUPLE

&

Raking the pile of mulch, Rigo uncovers
two fat yellow hornets. Thick as slugs,
heavy with poison, they barely manage
to fly—

&

Eddie in the garden, photographing bees.

&

when I picked him up, his limbs were hard
like something frozen. I felt the gas and fluids
stretching his gray tummy

&

Rigo waits till Eddie falls asleep, then slips
into the kitchen to masturbate. Whacking
his cock against the table, trying to hurry. Once
the neighbor boy came home late: headlights
jouncing through the window: caught.

What did he think he saw?

*

". . . A roommate?" Eddie asks. "Or boyfriend?
Because either one is all right. . ."

*

Lewis in the kitchen telling how Eddie lied,
pretended to go out of town to visit his family
so he could be with Jason. This story told
after the funeral, while Rigo is in the next room.

*

HOUSEMATE TO SHARE

*

Ausencio on the bathroom tile. His eyes open.

*

The bird skull Rigo hung on the grape trellis,
slipping a nail through the little hole
where its spinal cord had been—

*

*couldn't find the shovel and had to ask Tom
across the street: "Not the white one?" and I said no,
not Miss Kitty*

*

Rigo dreams of hands made of ice: filling
latex gloves with water, hanging them in the freezer.
Wires bent inside the fingers. Peeling off
the gloves to photograph the hands, one poking
from a sleeve, arm upraised to shield his face—

⁂

Quilts heaped at the foot of the bed. Pile them on then take
them off again. More towels. Alternate acetomenophin/
ibuprofen every four hours. More water. Whatever
Rigo is going through, he knows that Eddie's part is worse.

⁂

GAY COUPLE SEEKS

⁂

"Your cat's dead." I looked up. "What?"
"In the bathroom—" and then he was throwing up. . .

⁂

Now he feels sick touching himself.

⁂

Mother holding his hand as his heart stopped—

⁂

They glisten in the live oak: fingers dangling,
dripping: they disappear into earth, air.

⁂

Rigo holding Jason in the corridor: "This is real, isn't it?"

⁂

HOUSEMATE/LOVER

What's left?

⸏

Rigo's chest hurts. He's afraid his heart
will start pounding crazily like it did two weeks ago:
He couldn't sit up, couldn't reach the phone. The absurdity
of croaking beside Eddie in their bed . . .

⸏

104 and still rising. Make it stop.

⸏

No, don't.

LATE TESTAMENT

What are the birds?
Gray, gray as slate.

No, what are the birds?
Little scraps of pity.

What are they doing?
Clasping too tightly.

What do they tell you?
It's already too late.

What do you answer?
My tongue is too narrow.

What does that mean?
The birds understand.

How does the tree feel?
Terribly burdened.

How do you know this?
It's not what she planned.

What are they doing?
Collecting as one thought.

What does it look like?
An animate blanket—

What does the tree feel?
This loss will be harder—

You mean when the birds go?
Yes, when the birds go.

All as one garment
all in one motion

they mimic the body,
its copied form flung into air—

Who could endure such a thing?

ARRIVAL

When Christ came back
no one was prepared, not even Aunt Sally,
a hardened Baptist who had the good grace
to witness Christ slide down a chute of light

onto her swimming pool. He stepped
across, knocked politely at the kitchen door.
Sally's mouth swung open. She'd been snapping
beans, a bushelful she'd bought at the farmer's

market that morning. The canning jars rattled,
boiling on the stove. Christ pointed to his Timex,
tapped the crystal. *Je-je-just a minute,* Sally
stammered, reeling in the kitchen, switching off

the stove. She yanked at her apron. Should she leave
a note for Bob? *Excuse me?* Christ said, his voice
like grainy honey. Sally whirled, surprised to find
her body slumped among the beans.

FOLLOWING LORCA

He leads me down the wet avenue, his black coat flapping,
like the boatman he oars us through the rainy city, shiny taxis
skim past in humming slow motion, trains rumble below
the streets, muted thunder moans from the grates, he wants
to show me something, his white shirt flashes like his teeth,
the thin wince I take for a smile, his slick black hair shines
like an accident, I'm lost or high or dreaming, I recognize
his face, those bruised eyes, the rain, each drop
displaces its companions as a crowd gives way
for a celebrity, half-touching, half-parting, ringed kisses
that open and open, we drift toward the river, the bridge lights
crinkle in the water, I know his wound, he wants me there,
he doesn't have to ask, when he turns to unlock his mouth
I'm ready with my tongue, with my whole drowning heart.

HAIR

There is a house painted white. There is a tree,
its trunk painted the same white. There is a dog on a chain
tangled around the tree. There is a yard but it is all dirt,
worn smooth by the dog and the girl. The girl kneels
in the dirt, singing. She is washing doll clothes in a bucket.
Stuck in the fence beside her are the dolls, their pink
scrubbed bodies drying. Their heads poked through
the chainlink fence. Hanging by their hair, little Absaloms,
little Barbies, little perfect feet. She holds one doll
under the water. Promise you won't tell, she sings,
and I'll let you go. She squeezes the doll in her fist;
little bubbles leak from its neck. Promise. Hurry up.

PEG OF MY HEART

Peg of my heart, flap
of my ear, hinge of my knee,

pan of my brain. Blue
of my eye, ball of my hip,

curve of my frown, sack
of my bones. Box of my voice,

coil of my gut, flake
of my scalp, pearls of my teeth.

Spring of my step, fall
of my pride, pad of my toe,

swell of my cock—love
of my life, one day, all this will be yours.

THE SOUND

I'm digging in the garden when I hear it, an inhuman grating,
a wrenching moan and I think it's an injured child and drop
my shovel and step into the street to look, the kind of sound

a dog might make in grief, my neighbor's unloading something
from his truck, the tailgate's open and there's this awful keening
as he carries boxes back and forth, it's the rusted hinges rubbing

but I can't let go of it, the sound the body would make in protest,
and I've slipped from the school bus steps, landed on my back
on the rainy pavement, everything collapses, my body buckling

and unbuckling, trying to force air back into my lungs, I stagger
up the walk like a long blackening tunnel toward the school,
my vision flickering, this horrible sound engulfing me, a human

accident, a body wreck, a wracking shuddering bass, Diana
Winterberger pounding me on the back, screaming *He can't
breathe!* as people swirl around me, I'm parting my classmates

like a messenger with terrible news, and Neal Brandenburg,
the school punk, turns from his locker with a sour *I always said
that kid was queer*, and Mr. Dennison, the coach, is running

toward me as I pivot halfway up the stairs and everything
goes black and the next moment I'm in his downstairs office,
he's leaning over me, I'm listening for that sound and only then

understand it had been coming out of me, his face is close to mine,
I think of his nickname, Peachy, the boys in gym class say he can't
grow a beard, *I'm sorry*, I say, *It's not your fault*, he says, *What

happened*, he says, and I want to ask him what that other boy
was talking about, *I fell off the bus*, what did it mean, *I hit my back*,
and he helps me sit up and asks if he can lift my shirt to look,

I can't believe his hands could touch me and not hurt, but I nod,
there in the pocket of quiet surrounding us both.

CLARK
PHILIP F.

twice shy

Philip F. Clark is the author and editor of *The Artpoint*, a weblog that presents the work of emerging and established artists. He recently co-curated the exhibition "Inside Out: Portraiture Today" at the Watchung Arts Center in New Jersey. Also an artist, his collages and digital art have been exhibited at Climate/Gallery in New York. He participated in a forthcoming documentary on the paintings of Branden Charles Wallace called "The Comfort of Men," soon to be released by Magus Pictures, Inc.

theartpoint.blogspot.com

LEARNING

Put up your fists,
my father said.
And so I did.
So I have been
ever since;
I've won
nothing, gained less.
Blood weary,
well-worn,
I resist what I can.
Father,
what did you think
I would learn?
That the heart,
with an uppercut
had fists in return?
The swarm cheers
the down-turned
thumb. Be a man, he said,
and so I've tried.
Fight like a man, he said.
I've loved men
like a man
instead.

WANT

You enter me with spotless grammar.
What I love most is the instant just before I touch
you—
before flesh feels what the eye has longed for.

BREATHE

Breathe, you said,
breathe—
as you took my breath away
entering more than my body
while calling my name.

Sweat for lube, breathless
sweet unrest.
Kiss me you said,
and I gave you
breath,
instead.

Alone, later
my body wept,
though dry-eyed I
just glanced ahead.
What can loving do,
which calls us back
and fails the
promise kept.

WATCH

This tangle of sweat and grunt
this scrum of tongues, this yell,
this hope, this hell,
this urgent bed of sighs.
This peace, this kiss
of kind to kind.
This clock, this night,
this nothingness,
this hallowed sky of sex;
this sleep, this thought,
this happiness
under a moon of
knowing eyes.

THE CHANCES

So this is it,
the hit or miss
of life my love:
a change of planes,
the bus, the car, the knife;
the leap, the kiss.
The cry.
We live on
borrowed time,
We lie embraced but alone.
It's never what we wished,
it's always what we had,
and glad for hope
we borrowed more.
The chance,
the smile, the razor eye,
the marble neck and
the humble pie.

DEFINITE CHARACTER

Not far away,
just distant enough.
Not at arm's length,
just not eye to eye.

What is the measure
between us now?
And what to measure by:
the silences or the storms;

the peace at night
or the absence of arms?
Your face is no map;
it is a country I have no tongue for.

MORNING PIECE

The angers are over,
I've shouted my last.
The sun is about to rise. I shave,
make the coffee, butter the bread.
Still wet and wanting
the day begins;
the lights enter shadows like friends.
Every object colors
a thought, and slowly
I forgive.
You, fast asleep.
How could I not love this much,
looking at you now
as I leave for work—
me in my suit and you
in your sunlight and dreams.

THE OTHER LIFE

The other life
is the other kiss
when I am kissing you;
the second thought,
and the second skin.

The other life
is gladly lived—
a sleepwalk through
dreams in the waking hours;
life on the cusp, on the quiet,
on the down low,
just out of reach
and always at hand.

The other life
lies just below the surface;
vagrant, itinerant,
unsighted and seen.
Two great loves
in one life, now
three.

The other life
is watched and waiting;
has a mouth of glass
and eyes of stone.

The other life
is charred with time;
the clock untouched,
and watched by
an untroubled eye.

SENTINELS

Was that love?
Then what is this?
Dormant robes
in crimson disarray,
the crisping song of flags.
A lone metal heel step,
one hammer count. The cold snap.
One last match on a windy day.

If that was love,
then what remains?
Shoeless dream walker ill at ease.
Beside myself with hope. Beside myself.

Can this be love?
Then what do I know?
The stitch, the rosary, the marine in the rain.
Ferocious change, abundant spies.

This is love.
A thousand chances in a day.
Auguries abound, tallies are kept.
The sullen stare of the lemon moon.
With perfect pitch, love is what remains.

THE BREAK

The night
you broke
up with me,
with
your

        quiet,

           slow,

                enormous

No,
I heard
chandeliers

        breaking

            falling

in palaces
long since gone.
In all that din
you held me,
to listen
to the rain
of glass
and dreams.
The rooms
in which
I answered
now

      empty,

         dark,

           soundless.

Clean.
And what I answered was
Yes
to you,
and the break of
glass that holds me here.

SODEN
CHRISTOPHER

just the rough moon and us

Christopher Stephen Soden is a writer, teacher, critic, lecturer, performer, and a native Texan. He received his MFA in Writing (Poetry) from Vermont College in January of 2005. He was a film critic for *The Fort Worth Ally* and currently writes theatre critique for John Garcia's *The Column* and *Examiner.com*. In 2007, "Queer Anarchy," a performance piece he wrote, received *The Dallas Voice*'s People's Voice Award for Best Stage Performance. In August 2010 he received a full fellowship to Lambda Literary's Retreat for Emerging LGBT Voices in Los Angeles, California. His work has appeared in *Ganymede, Gay City 2, Poetic Voices Without Borders, The Texas Observer, Sentence, Borderlands, Cafe Review, Velvet Mafia, Poetry Super Highway, Gertrude, Touch of Eros, ArLiJo, Windy City Times, Best Texas Writing 2*, and elsewhere. Of the poems published here, "the hand i was dealt" appeared in *Poetry Super Highway, Velvet Mafia*, and *ArliJo*, "Drive-In Movie" appeared in *Illya's Honey*, "because they are not eight" appeared in *Everything I Have Is Blue*, and "Closer" and "Alphadog" appeared in *Polari Journal*.

ALPHA DOG
for Nate

From the very beginning something
about Nate really set me off,
hearing him talk with the others
about women. There was a shift
in tone. It wasn't leering or salacious,
but angry like, like a seething
geyser, or subtle poison swimming
the stream of their male blood.
Now of course I'm a guy,
and probably not especially
enlightened. But he struck me as
a dolt. I would chuckle too
when the women found names
for him they would never speak
to his face. But who could blame
them, when Nate would target one
with his swagger and cooly-cool
disaffection, like he was the only one
audacious enough to bring desire
into the conversation? *You know*
you want me. He knew the value of
his stock. The dark wavy curls,
the lean raw rough appeal of his
slender nose, flush and freckle
of his strong burly jaw. I remember
him flashing his milky ass when he
and Sarah swam the cold Adriatic,
diving to give me the full benefit.
Yeah he knew I was a queerboy.
We were all MFA students and nobody
cared, though for all the repulsion
he stoked in me, he took it in stride.
He kissed me at the New Year's Dance
without missing a beat and there were
times when I thought we understood
each other better than anyone
in our own tribe. One cold groggy

Vermont morning as I lumbered
into the men's toilets I found the stall
next to him. It was easy to recognize
his pajama trousers and I greeted
him, chipper and exhilarated, as if
I could see past the partitions
dividing us, and he, again without
hesitation, cracked wise about amenities,
Why couldn't they find softer paper?

THAT DAY

He came home with a coloring book
handing it to me without a word,
his face slack with resignation
and fatigue, his shirt damp with blotches
of sweat. He was somehow more present
than I can recall before or since. Mother,
sensing my confusion, explained,
"The dentist pulled Daddy's teeth
to make room for dentures. He cannot speak
or have dinner with us." How could a boy
so small grasp the gravity of an event
that has suddenly taken the weight
of sacrament? The distance in my mother's
voice, the solitude as my dad removed
coat and tie, settling into his chair and unfolding
the evening paper. How could a simple mistake
knock the revolving and chaotic globe from its
axis? How could two sentient mammals drift
so far from one another and beyond
repair? I can only tell you I remember
a flood of sadness for a father I do not think
I liked. The profound lack of understanding
of why he made the trip to the grocery store
to buy me a gift, on a day that must have been
so awful for him. I cannot believe it
has taken me fifty-two years to stumble
upon this epiphany. I cannot believe I'm telling
you that I love him.

HANGING

there were girls along too when I was
15 traveling in a group called young
church men from parish to parish restoring
shingles or paint jobs or gardens hosting
folk masses and potluck dinners where
we sang about god made flesh and shared
in a supper of bread and wine and molecules
juxtaposed at st francis in orangeville the boys
hung a sheet over a clothesline and all washed
together great lathering with other hairy-assed
guys pissing and joshing and looking for once
without dread or feeling like a copperhead
sleeping next to them delighting in the music
of their breath cutting black waves
on lake michigan at midnight in a speedboat
just the rough moon and us

CLOSER

returning to your room
on the men's floor to hear
water your best friend
borrowing your shower
explaining his is broken
and the two of you so close
he knew you wouldn't mind
grinning rambunctiously
his voice bounces
as if through a bottle
curtain pulled halfway back
his crooked wattled dick
curving downward
like a hook his piss
escaping in a careless jet
completely at ease with you
winking drops glisten
from nose earlobes suds
adorning wilted hair
of ass cleft what exactly
is he offering is he
the brother you never had
do you believe you know
the difference between
recognition and epiphany
is this grace or is he
unapproachable
as God how exactly
do you connect
exhale or surrender
or horseplay if you ask
to compare or climb in
got room for me bro
will it ever be
the same

THE SAILOR'S COMPANION
after Pound

When my folks still got me buzzcuts and capguns
I would climb the magnolia, lolling in close perfume.
You rode by on a gleaming *Schwinn*, howling
Blue Suede Shoes, circled my tree like a coyote.
We both lived in the small town of Waxahachie.
Two boys who knew nothing about each other.
At 20 you pulled me over and kissed me.
Too shy to reciprocate, or object
I turned my head, asked for the speeding ticket.
You called and called. Left a thousand messages.

At 21 my grin broke, finally, through.
I wanted your tears and mine to mix
Forever and forever and forever.
Why should I look for a wife?

At 22 you enlisted.
Stationed at Camp Lejeune, northeast of Myrtle Beach.
You've been gone half a year now
The coyotes serenade me nightly.

Your boots dragged when you left
The backyard a jungle of spider lily and mallow
Too dense for me to clear!
Early autumn leaves float the wind.
Hummingbirds back too soon from migration
Hover and mingle at our feeders.
I cannot bear to look. I'm getting old, Sam.
If you go fishing along the shores of Cape Fear
And let me know just where.
I can hitchhike if you want me
All the way to Lillington.

BECAUSE THEY ARE NOT EIGHT

Ronnie started talking to me when
they were shearing us in bunches, clumps
of sandy brown, black, and rusty hair
splotching dingy yellow linoleum. Heaping
in small drifts. Some trippy inane shit he said
made me laugh though I couldn't tell you why.
My precious mane! My masculine fortitude!
Like some kind of eulogy for Caesar.

I never thought of it as mine anymore
after it was cut. And you always get more.
We bunked together. Closed the taverns in port.
They gave us watch duty on deck beginning
an hour before the next day. Creaming
night waves were ragged claps of wet
voltage teasing your mind into a graceful

stupor. It was steady and soothing and Ronnie
and me would unwind. Nothing mattered
to him I think. The way a lost balloon
meanders and bobs. Tangles and glides. Ronnie
asked me why sometimes sailors are called gobs.
I said he should ask the captain. He cradled
my neck, hooking his lips into mine.

I caught him with a rabbit punch and he yelped
and bayed. Shaking back to his feet with raucous
guffaws he kissed me again with blood in his
mouth. I spat into the hollow of his chest
and cried some, socking his shoulders and arms.
I said, "It's okay for you first," and he got in

after three fingers and rubbed my belly whispering,
singing Sinatra (Summer Wind) and I was frail
and genuine suddenly under hushy symphony
of leaking light, thinking of my grandma's riddle:
Why are the seven stars no more than seven?
I don't mind if he wakes me for a slip trip

'cause I get my chance at bat as often
as I like. Ronnie can turn cook's duty for three
hundred guys into a fucking privilege. Swabbing
toilets a jokey tango for the deranged. Sometimes
he just climbs into my bunk and tells me gags
'til we fall asleep. I do not ask God why

He brought me Ronnie. Prince of tickles
in a kingdom of the damaged and ravenous.
Doctor for the annihilated bounce. I heard
once in church deserving has nothing
to do with grace. And I figure it's better
not to raise the question.

NEIGHBOR
for MG

His hair is dark and impeccably
smooth, in the dissolving pools
of gray and yellow light
when he comes out for a cigarette.
He wears a sleeveless undershirt
even when the temperature drops,
and I can see the paddles
of his ceiling fan wheel urgently
through the open doorway
one story up and across
from my patio. Tonight he is
leaning against the iron railing,
his gaze taking him farther
than windows, leaves, and clouds.
His eyes glisten like a raccoon's,
or a coyote's, though probably
not as reflective as he appears,
in this moment when I am
privileged to share
the reverie of what could be
recollection, rumination or wish.
For the first time music escapes
his living room. Favorite band
of a girl I can never forgive.
Even from where I sit he has
the cast of a Latino or Italian
and though his chin could be
stronger, I would welcome him
into my arms, my mouth.
We take a slow luxurious
draw on our smokes, inspiration
guiding careless focus.
Don't worry buddy. I will not
divulge our indiscretion.
Whether we are secret brothers,
lovers, or something in-between,
this now is mine and endless,
and will follow me on that long
last river crossing to bliss.

DRIVE-IN MOVIE

I like your baby blue convertible,
luster and dazzle of its chrome
flanks and jewelry, combustible
chariot of locomotion, cloud chaser
you arrive in to collect me. I climb
aboard, drown in the stereo bop
and cool cool yes yes careening
from the jazz riffs and licks, while
rough wind teases and buffets our hair.
Doesn't matter what's playing tonight
cause it's enough just having you
this close. Behind the screen the canvas
is seven stories high, makes me think
of days before I was an itch,
when my folks came here, egg-paint
picture of the circus with its clowns
and ponies and tigers and acrobats.
Acrobats can spin and stretch and dive
and land back on their feet just so,
they fly and diminish the space between
them until they inevitably connect.
The sun is going down as we pay
and hook the speaker on your door.
Watermelon pink evening sky
suffuses and darkens: now cranberry,
raspberry, dewberry, huckleberry, plum.
Trailer music kicks in: Kiss kiss bang bang.
Night air warm and plausible flows
like tides of blood that pound and tick
within us, tainting our skin. I have
brought vodka mixed with crushed
lemon and sugar and ice and cut
the strong peel into strips.
It goes down really nice. Your scent

steeps and billows, coats my neck
and arms. "Baby, what are we gonna
do? Will we make it out alive?
Wait wait wait wait wait. Lemme think."
Chuckles bubble between us slow
and languid. Mosquitoes probe and tap
my arms as I tap you. Your mouth
is sour, smoky, scalding. The stars
and crickets, they turn, they turn
away.

THE HAND I WAS DEALT

i knew you in halls and tawdry yellow gloss
of first school days ashen sky of recess
before i understood words like *queer sissy faggot*
bruiser too cool for smarts while i failed
to comprehend the history of our transaction:
fathers conferring failure upon sons and sons
transmitting futility to other sons of living
up to our dicks repugnance of thinking
another boy had anything for you the hand
withdrawn the other lad forever backing away
smiling you spat the words of estrangement
before realizing i had made some kind of choice
i might say the clock and personal witness
have only vindicated me though what to make
of your clammy paw priming my languid manhood
under god's cold mercury vapor angels
in parking lot of cruise park and rest
stop i could not begin to say

SAX SAM

a molotov press conference

Sam Sax is a queer jewish cissy-gendered poet living in the Bay Area and currently is a part of the Bay's literary and slam scenes. He toured the country for a year in an aqua saturn with a poetics collective called *...we are the Unreal* which appeared at countless slams, open mics, universities, basements, and queer glitter festivals. He's got a handful of chapbooks and CDs and is currently working on his first book, *Hella Gay Notes from Underground.*

www.facebook.com/samsax

FROM MONSTERO.S STOMACH

i never wanted to be a real boy

i was born with a two by four for a sternum
woodchip on my shoulder
driftwood for legs
and matchsticks hidden in these fingertips
it seems i have always been destined to burn

trapped in my mother.s belly
something woman and blue
hid life inside of my tinderbox gut
barely the size of a whisper
as she breathed this firewood
form into bloom

i am told they all thought
i was such an empty and beautiful child
a hand puppet waiting to be filled

so they would tell me
cautious as a chainsaw.s
bite into bark

samuel,
you will one day grow into a man
now you are still too gentle with the dirt
too god and sex in the same word
men are hard as petrified forests
they do not soften in the rain

so in classrooms i learned how to
carve my name into the faces of plywood desks
how to not look away as i tore into its flesh
always jealous of the ease with which these
other boys seemed to fit into their bodies

no hinges where their joints should be
no strings tied at the wrists

those rock and scissor boys
forever burning woodchips on the playground

i never wanted to be them

i am told
men are dogwood made.
we are played by the hands
of a world that never knew how to hold us
are meant to make marionettes out of women
play heart strings like handcuffs

there is a fire in the wild eyes
of a boy who knows he will one
day grow to become manacles
my desire has always been to
find a way for them to fill my softness
fuck me 'til i am rosewood paper
cut my strings 'til i am tree rings in their chest
it seems i have always been destined to burn

trapped in the belly of a whale
i met my maker, his hands held the touch
of redwood and resembled my own.
his legs also driftwood

and beneath the cathedral
of the beast.s rib bone.s rafters
he told me cautious as slash and burn

samuel,
you were such an empty and beautiful child
what have you let yourself become filled with?
you are still too gentle with the dirt/still soften in the rain
you have grown into the shape of a man
without root or veins
each gesture i have painted onto your skin
is empty performance
grow your bark until it covers
all of your silence
hide inside the shadows of your body
learn to speak gasoline
never have any children

you will not know how
to teach them to be men

i am a special puppet
one who never wanted to be real
one who will be performing his whole life.

I.D.Z, EROS, AND SUPERHERO.S

i saw an octopus
pregnant with television wires
clinging to the side of a brick building,

a man blows his shofar
into the hollow of a dumpster

and a car
filled with nothing but light
drives through darkness

sometimes this world
does not make sense

at the corner of alabama
and cesar chavez there is
a contradiction

a condominium made of skin
climbing sideways out of
the pavement

growing toward the shadows
of police lights. eating oxygen
and the freshest canned vegetables
from the corner store.

the structure.s key corner stone
is a human tooth covered in gold
mined by the hands of forty-niners
hands wet with the blood of newly spanish mouths

there is a mural in an alleyway
that portrays this monster of capitalism
lurking in the foundations,
claiming buildings for limbs
and pig.s revolvers for tongues
that speak dollar sign and breath eviction.

at the intersection
of hipster and human

there is a dance hall
made from the body
of a converted nazi bunker

at night. german children
dance their grandparent.s
dances to music made by
the descendants of auschwitz

now the bible tells us that
it took white jesus
seven days to colonize
san francisco.

at the intersection
of hipster and human

there is a dance hall
made from the body
of an old spanish church
of a methadone clinic
of a santaria ritual site

at night, white children
fill its belly with black music
and dance whiskey lullabies to bedlam

children dressed
in their grandparents prejudice
press dollar bills into the barrels
of riot cop guns

then run home safe as a house
to plant flowers in the mouths
of gated gardens

it is here i saw a church bell shaped
like a fist

a molotov press conference
occupying the silence of a
repossessed stairwell

and a car filled with nothing
but police light profiled in darkness

most times this world
it does not make sense

at the corner of alabama
and cesar chavez there is
a contradiction.

i live near here
on a border.s edge
paying a border.s rent
for four walls and a floor
as dirty as my mind is.

at night my neighborhood
is a beehive filled with high
fructose corn syrup

it is a syringe injected into
the limb of a city park tree

duct tape handcuffs placed on the
mouth of a river paying dowry
to this hungry city
that never
lets it
sleep

FOR HART CRANE:
ON THE 78TH ANNIVERSARY OF HIS DEATH
AND ON MY FIRST LEARNING THAT HE HAD EVER LIVED

the bottom of the sea is cruel - hart crane

before our worlds turn
into wormholes

and our typewriter.s block
builds a death sentence
into our young queer hearts

spelling our self destruction
giant big across that silent sky

you word spoke an antihero poetics
through a broken telephone
to nowhere

borrowed a lesser pen
to stroke the paper grid
into accepting your ink

think there is no place
for square pegs like us, hart
i know this

this sinkhole decoder ring future
depuzzle the present and jigsaw
through what remains

blame the world
for not letting you
fit into it neat enough
for never letting you
write the waste land happy

our tamed tongues
our borrowed parting words

in the accident that followed
your final speech act
you sight sang a swan song to
a life that looked more like
a pigeon park dance party
than any first flight

suicyanide swallow
all your poems till your gut busts
book binding thick

this is a reason to write
this is a reason to live

get dead then get published
weren.t you curious
how your life would be read
by a world that might curl
your every word around their tongue?
that could love you as much as you hated
yourself

they have erected your golden
statute of limitations
in a parking meter.s playground
feeding coins into capital mouths
waiting for your work to expire
waiting for you to run out

but you were born with
a silver gun in your mouth
and have spent your whole
life expecting to make love to
that trigger
never knew the splatter
paint ricochet would
leave you here
empty in the cannons of
children.s curriculum systems
stiff in teachers rulers
chalk outlined on the washed whiteboard
basically invisible
but still bursting through the surface

i too have had to learn to speak
cursive in order to hide better
in my words

i too understand what it is like
to live in a world where our love
letters are read as ransom notes

tell me hart,
was your new york
on the horizon when you
spoke your final opus
said "goodbye, everybody"
then dove head first into the
gulf of mexico never to resurface

you deep sank quick
into quick sand sleep

died in the same history thick waters
where all queer writers go to rest in peace

know our love has never been cheap
know our poems know how to code switch in their sleep
know that beneath the cold salt water ocean
is an auditorium packed past fire code
waiting to hear you speak

SPEECH ACTOR

there is a place
hidden in the crook
of my throat that i never
speak from.

bricked up behind
every theft my tongue
has ever committed to memory

dialects spelling out
the street level window
of a house broken into

stole the silver lining
from their heirloom.s chest
and for a time used it as my own

sometimes my speech acts violently
it is a pirate posing as anthropologist
waiting to dig up someone.s family.s bones
only for the purpose of better building
my own story arc.

i picked up a twang
after living in Atlanta
for two days.

a midwestern drawl
as i arrived at the Cleveland
busport

and now somehow my talk.s
hella bay

i know there is no tapedeck
that can record this confession.

so for today, i will break the brick
layers hands and heal them into ciphers.

unlock the safe in my voice box
and speak honest for the first
time in this counterfeit life.

it will sound something like this

    [silence]

BED.BUGZ

if sleep is the cousin of death
then death must be
my schizophrenic cousin daniel
who reads talmud
claims our family are direct descendants of god

and sleep
drinks alone in bathrooms
claims his brain cells are not destroyed
they are merely expanded

this is how we get through the night:
kiss the backhand of a bottle of bourbon
drink aerosol spit shine through a loaded pen
eat a fistful of vicodine for breakfast
fist fuck a church door.s wood mouth

this is how we. this is how we.
this is how we get through the night

awoke on a pillow of my own vomit
recall how stripped concrete sheets
had made a bed for me in the mansion
of my madness. my mouth a bloody
grin after dining on a banquet of pavement.

watch how men
dressed in burial suits
walk slow in morning
toward a punch clock
feeding days to their paychecks

children back home with mouths
hungry as fresh graves

from broken condom
to broken promise

that morning
daylight straight razored my gay nightlife

and i wished i hadn.t told bedtime to go fuck herself
that walk home i thanked my lucky now hidden stars
that i had no one to come back to

this is how we get through the night
after i left my last lover broken in an adjacent bedroom
when we learned that our words would
not help us remember how to speak to each other again
he asked me 'how i sleep at night'
naked as countless sheep i told him:
nightly baptisms in a bottles of bourbon
writing until my knuckle bleeds into the table
an alarm clock shaped like a fistful of pills
and cursing god as often as i remember he does not exist

always fearful of waking a sleeping giant
i have learned to fall in love how i fall asleep
as fucked up as possible

this is how we. this is how we
this is how we…
if daniel was right
and my family are actually direct descendants of god
and if children learn to smile from their fathers
than god must have a grin like a cemetery
with tombstone teeth
pointing forward always forward
to that second cousin of sleep

but i learned how to cheat the night from my mother
cups of hot black morning resting like an infant in her palm
i wonder if i envied their closeness
if i learned to nurture my insomnia like a child
let it grow inside of me until
i birthed nightmares onto my bed sheets

in my house we only found rest at the end
of a deadened nerve ending
after emptying these coffee can heads
and letting us fill again with stripped wool
and feathers

when my mother found me
a carcass lying on the carpet next to the bed like a bleeding lamb
with everything possible stripped down to empty
she asked me if i ever felt like my cousin daniel
and i told her through gritted gravestone teeth

mom.
we are all just searching for ways to finally
rest in peace.

SIEK
ROBERT

hiding from nothing

Robert Siek has been featured in *Swallow Your Pride*, *Dwan*, *Bay Windows*, *The Rogue Scholars Collective*, *The Columbia Poetry Review*, *Lodestar Quarterly*, *Unpleasant Event Schedule*, *Velvet Mafia*, *Court Green*, *Limp Wrist*, and *Mary: A Literary Quarterly*. In 2001, Wayne Koestenbaum selected his manuscript as the winner of the New School Chapbook Award Series, and the New School published his chapbook *Clubbed Kid* in the spring of 2003. Four of his poems appear in the anthology *Cat Breath: A Rogue Scholars Two-Headed Kitty Anthology* (Rogue Scholars Press, 2005). His short story "Sixteen" was published in the fiction anthology *Userlands: New Fiction Writers from the Blogging Underground*, edited by Dennis Cooper and published by Akashic Books (January 2007).

BANDSTAND BOYS, FOOTBALL PLAYERS, AND GREASERS

part one

Dusting my cologne bottles, dropping my right shoulder
and raising the left to each beat of the The Jelly Beans
singing "I Wanna Love Him So Bad," filling my head
with 1964, a decade before I was born, three girls
dancing in sync wearing floral pattern dresses,
buns wrapped high, little hoop earrings, big smiles
covering their faces like a number one hit
was in the works. And I picture the boys
cheering them on like black and white
Bandstand, so American like Dick Clark
asking questions about the future and how bright
it is. They mash potato with clinking knees, sweating
beneath plaid chinos, neck ties flapping like dog tongues
licking carpets or kitties cleaning paws. Johnny's top button
pops off, and he loosens the knot. Jeanie flaps her dress harder
spying chest hairs peeking out of his undershirt at the indent
where his neck ends and the sternum begins. Someone
yells "Come on baby!" and Ellie yells "let's do the twist!"
The dance floor rumbles like tectonic plates shifting
underground, teenage earthquake, hips bounce
like bumper cars banging and spinning,
like real car accidents, 360s on the highway.

BANDSTAND BOYS, FOOTBALL PLAYERS, AND GREASERS

part two

I spritz Gucci Envy in the air, sniffing
the masculine musk that creeps invisible
like post-scrimmage steam—hot showers
in a gym locker room. A high-school football team
is everywhere. I'm naked and seated. They shout
and slam helmets, opening locker doors, passing
padlocks and benches. Photos of seniors in uniforms
standing shoulder to shoulder flash and pop, like flipped pages
in my mother's 1963 yearbook—aged pages that released scents
And I'm touching my hips, Jimmy and Larry undress next to me.
One bends over like stretching for calisthenics, toe touches
before a game, sliding his jock strap from waist to ankles.
I bend forward and watch the dark line
extending from the curve of his back,
dividing his ass, where hair collects,
twisted grass growing from a crack in a driveway.
Odors hit like pollution, almost leaving me unconscious,
and Larry wipes his removed jersey over his bare chest,
saying "good game," while scratching his ass.
He splashes some of his father's aftershave, palm to cheeks,
telling Jimmy how he snatched it, something from dad's medicine cabinet.
Natural body odor and artificial musk mount
beneath my nostrils and hump.
I squeeze my hard-on thigh to thigh,
bunching a towel over pubes and balls,
hiding it all, and picture a male dog shove its snout between its legs
grunting like a pair of raccoons mating behind trash cans.

BANDSTAND BOYS, FOOTBALL PLAYERS, AND GREASERS

part three

"Leader of the Pack" blasts from my boom box.
I place the cologne bottle back on the shelf,
listening to two Shangri-Las ask the third
about a new greaser boyfriend.
They sing and motorcycles rev;
I sit at my desk in a swivel chair.
I become a doctor in a high-school nurse's office.
Boys wearing leather jackets are led in,
dressed in white T-shirts and tight blue jeans.
The nurse pulls a curtain around us.
The young men form a line and face forward,
something military, ready to fight—unbuttoning,
unzipping, lifting their armor, waiting to be checked
for battle wounds, injuries, areas of infection.
Denim unwraps down hairy legs, dragging boxers
to the floor: fabric ovals rest like fetters over feet,
like prisoners of war, my hostages.
I glance from one end to the other, make mental notes
on adolescent stages. The most matured one at center
is five inches flaccid. I roll in, still seated,
and slip into his personal space, feeling heat,
lava raining over my head from a volcano erupting
on a tropical island. He hangs an arm's length from my face.
I grasp his scrotum, my fingers behind his set. Warmth pours molten
through my grip, over my arm like urine running down a leg in winter.
He twitches within my cold clutch, something expected from the medical,
and his pubes tickle my palm, like palm trees shaking against the sky
when the ground becomes unsteady, the earth's crust unbalanced,
earthquakes and volcanoes destroying small towns
like dance halls exploding with trumpets alerting, skirts flaring,
and hands clapping over the music, like shoulder pads digging through
freshly cut grass as boys dive for footballs fumbled near the 10-yard line,
or greasers smashing beer bottles on garbage cans in alleys.
Inside, cologne bottles sparkle on my desk
and my girl group CD spins to its end.
The Shangri-Las fade out, like streaks on cleaned glass
or raccoon eyes staring as headlights flash past.

HOME

Rental in a three-story building,
I'm gonna blast the *Wiz* soundtrack,
imagine I have doors, knobs.
Windows open, all options, cartwheels
past moving traffic. No one heeds STOP signs.
It's a double-dog dare for a single gay man,
weekend nights searching craigslist personal ads,
slide some oil to me, men seeking men,
only in the neighborhood. Color me danger,
the sex and excitement, what comes after
bed death in a long-term relationship,
no nude couple for too many years.
Time to suck multiple cocks, *ease on down the road,*
relearn, unlock. Because *you can't win, child,*
but you can hook up, late night,
following e-mails, pics of a hard-on, a face,
a rundown of likes, dislikes, hosting or traveling.
My buzzer doesn't work; so text or call
outside my home, I'll fetch you in seconds,
pull back my comforter. Yes I'm clean,
fingers, soap, scrubbed feet, no deodorant.
It's deep, armpits open game. *So tell me,*
what, what would I do if I could feel
your hand on the back of my head,
my knees bending as I squat between your legs.
You sit on the couch jerking for show.
Well I'm a mean, old lion, and the hunt is over,
his pants peeled from beneath buttocks, skin and fur
stretched and snapped from fresh carcass.
He likes his ass eaten, turning, raising it
and spread, all fours, exposing pink of insides,
the folds my tongue befriends. Road kill reanimated,
filling underwear, STOP signs run down, shove it farther,
it's a brand new day, an accident at every corner,
a bottle of lube, a condom unrolled.
Is this what feeling gets? Pre-cum on my belly;
some people stare out windows.
This is my new apartment in a three-story building,

the *Wiz* soundtrack closing from computer speakers.
He wants to come in my mouth. I ask him if it feels good,
the taste of used laytex. He's going to shoot, and *home
is knowing, if you believe.* It's a rental, temporary.
I'm kneeling on a towel. I tell him I swallow,
and finish what I started.

1979

Ten rows away from the back of the movie theater,
1979, my Dad and I watch *The Brood*. Mutant-face midgets
climb a kindergarten teacher, attacking her with toy hammers,
other colorful weapons. One figure hangs from her shoulders,
dressed in a down winter jacket. It's hood worn up.
Her face enlarged onscreen—even lipstick, Hollywood scream—
and blood spots are flicked like wet confetti. The teacher collapses.
Students stand watching. Red stains grow through her blue cotton dress;
small arms drum the life out of her, and maybe she was wearing
a brown wool blazer. I was five at the time.
The shot switches to her dead face,
and the mini-monsters leave with the main character's daughter.
I peer over the back of my seat, trying to see swinging doors
or the farthest back wall. Shapes are moving in the last row,
like ink spots on Rorschach tests—three dimensional, animated—
as though breathing under sheets, like inflated body bags,
filled with morgue storage, victims in horror movies.
I'm next to my father, so I worry for both of us.
This is the second time I witness this—the first during *Phantasm*,
the plot led to a funeral home, yellow blood squirting from a hand
following dismembered fingers and floating spheres of surgical steel
drilling into people's heads. I looked to my right every two minutes,
wondering when to duck. Headlights hit the windshield,
creating shadows on the dash. I'm alone in my father's work van,
sitting on a folded blanket in the back surrounded by auto glass
in racks and some bins filled with sealants, razors, and gloves.
It's early evening in the racetrack parking lot. Dad told me
to keep the doors locked. Our dog Baron sits in the passenger seat,
pony-sized with wiry brown and black hair, an Airdale terrier,
standing guard while Dad is gone. Another set of headlights flash inside,
and Baron watches something go by. I hear cars drive. He said
he'd be quick. I wanted to pick horses, place bets. Lights
invade again, like the moon dropped feet from the roof of the van
or a movie projector aimed overhead, focusing on the rear doors, exposing
airborne particles, like flashlights in dark hallways or torches
in castle corridors, lighthouses on mainland shores, or search parties
in forests pre-dawn—parents urging everyone to keep looking,
like horror movies didn't exist and locked doors
never really made a difference. An engine turns off,

no more floor lights in the aisles. I'm alone in a van,
picturing creatures, child-size and faceless, kidnapping kindergarteners,
blackness above me, behind me—ink stains bleeding on paper—
like trapped in a body bag, inflated, breathing.
I crawl up front behind the driver's seat, hiding from nothing.
Baron looks down at me, panting and wagging.

HANDBAGS

Jeff sits on a stool behind the cash register,
reading last month's copy of *Vogue*. He has
the latest *Interview* stashed under the fax machine
for when he's bored. There is a picture-window-sized poster
above his head, some Warhol-like image of a blonde woman
with painted-over-the-photo flesh-tone face, electric-blue eyes, yellow
spiraled hair, and red lips standing out on a hot-pink background.
Jeff stops skimming an article about Fall Fashion Week, turns, looks up,
and thinks *what does she have to do with handbags.* He spins back toward
the store entrance, glances at one wall and then the other. White walls
surround him, half-moon mirrors staggered on each side, reflecting French
handbags sitting on arc-shaped shelves, protruding like fungi on trees in a
forest—white discs stacked like steps to nowhere. Black leather bags that
look like plastic remain still under bright lights, collecting dust like beach
hats in the winter. There are mint green bags, coral colored bags, red ones,
periwinkle ones—a selection. Some bags are propped on 5-inch-high
stands on circular glass tables spread like bumpers inside pinball machines.
Jeff flips a few pages then sighs. He watches a fit Italian guy wearing a wife-
beater walk by. Two middle-aged black women pass in the opposite
direction. He looks at the wall again and notices the ceiling lights shining
off the display mirrors. Sunrises cross his mind, ones he watched with an
ex-boyfriend on Sunday mornings. People speed past the store entrance,
conversations following behind—couples holding hands, children running
while playing tag. Jeff notices someone in J. Crew waving at a stranger
standing in the mall—she's talking on a cell phone in front
of the store. A teenage kid in a hooded sweat jacket stops
in the walkway, takes a few steps inside, then yells "faggot"
as loud as he can. Jeff closes the magazine. The kid takes off
into the mall past security guards. Jeff jerks—nervous tic
like a crack in an ice cube popping in a glass of water. He sighs,
sits still, and then opens the magazine again, staring at words
but not reading them. The handbags continue to collect dust,
reflecting in half-moon mirrors that shine like lonely sunrises
somewhere in a mall in New Jersey.

PURPOSE AND DEVIL PISS

One out of four straight men appear nervous around me,
limp-wristed and reading a novel on the subway.

Certain it's not imagined, my days support this education,
stronger with years clean, a clear head aided by antidepressants.

I turn pages, content with fiction, brief travels backward
to recent moments on an off-white comforter, naked, panting,

a hand rubbing while I rock in minor jerks, legs spread
past his back, the guy I've been seeing this past month.

I come on his chest, an event earned, my knuckles numb,
thanks to overstretched fingers, red with my full weight,

a driven grip on a knife handle, Sadie saying hi from a hallway.
He said it was hot. Three weekends laughed in his studio apartment.

I lean back, lift my ass from his hips; his bed is dirt beneath me.
I'm Adam just created, with purpose, desire, the rediscovery

of fulfillment, a garden of options, plant life to name,
classify in books and offer to the public—

this is called ecstasy and these are five senses.
Another page turned, I look up a second.

A stare breaks, some male face avoiding,
fearful, like an X were carved in my forehead.

I no longer fantasize or read, but wonder why a stranger
cares how I judge him, godlike and punishing, a menace

in close quarters. Fuck this subway car, the people that share it.
We all stink in here, original sin bottled and sprayed,

a small army of foreign men, not with it, cologne bathed.
And last night on a couch in a nightclub,

I relaxed, his fingertips just inside my cut-off shorts,
part of a Halloween costume, a look from 1980; my yellow briefs,

slightly showing, as we discussed the weekend, the mutual joy
in time spent together. He joked that he doesn't mind

being my rebound. I said he was the furthest thing from it,
my previous long-term relationship buried out back,

beneath a garden, fertile earth soaked in life, devil piss.
I catch one out of four watching this kind living it—

too much to think about. I'm a Manson girl in protest,
shaved head and on all fours, demanding freedom for Charlie,

Xs cut into foreheads. I'll crawl till kneecaps crack
and scream so loud enemies drop dead. I have to finish this book,

text someone back; I'm the first man on earth,
no worries, no past.

DEVIL DOGS PERFORM

Bowls sticky with left-over milk—
cereal for dinner, the television turned on.
Uncle Don on-screen wearing a Latex glove,
telling a naked marine, "a hand is a hand son."

He films this, and others watch, sitting on towels
in unlit living rooms, circled by remotes and tissues,
and the scene is scanned forward to three 18-year-olds,
soldiers, tattoos of growling mongrels on upper arms;

"they call us Devil Dogs," one says. Uncle Don laughing,
"Show us those holes boys." Six legs over heads, stretches
in a gymnastics class, these boys on a king-size bed,
perhaps in Don's own home or a motel instead.

Close-ups of anuses, unicellular organisms,
covered in cilia, pink and still,
hiding between butt cheeks,
like three colored micrographs

in a biology textbook, 20,000 times life-size;
the filmmaker jokes about toilet paper; one actor
complains his hole is cold. Another says he'll warm it up.
Knees balance above while lower backs curl, cushioned

on a peach comforter. Scan again, the guy with the moustache
climbing buglike nowhere, pushing his dick deeper in his friend.
Don says, "a hole is a hole boy." Face bouncing at a bed corner;
he's blushing while taking it—his wedding ring showing.

"This hurts," he says. The third marine jams it
in his mouth. "That'll keep your mind occupied;
it's a big cock for the first time." Hands grab shoulders,
like no good footing next steps up; his whole weight drops

on his partner, this rock he tops. "What about that hole boy?"
He says, "it's tight," like the end of a marathon, the runner ready to fall—
"it's tight." This is a favorite instance, when a person out there shoots,
when Uncle Don yelps, "fuck that virgin hole," and the boy says,

"I can't do this anymore." "Fine, fine, sport," like giving up,
mid race, hands wave in universal stop gestures. His friend,
an insect clinging on, scurrying weightless on another human form,
jerking hips like unfinished dog business, when a puppy humps toys—

red rockets exposed. Pull out and zoom in, last shot of a wet protist,
cover slip off, the microscope raised up. This is gymnastics class ending,
last stretch, three Devil Dogs fast forwarded to ejaculating on one another.
Someone at home says, "tight," crumpling a tissue.

Cereal bowls still sticky, ass imprints in towels.
Uncle Don says, "thanks boys." T-shirts unfolded;
jeans pulled up. Someone hits Stop.
An apartment goes dark.

LIKE CLOCKWORK

My father calls my name up the staircase,
and I wake up at four in the morning,
like a door slammed or a glass broke—
my eyes opened—a robot switched on.
This isn't automatic; it's new, like combing
my hair in the opposite direction. He claims
that I have to drive him to the hospital.
His blood pressure is high. He woke up
drenched in sweat. These things scare him
since his heart attack seven weeks ago.
I sit up in bed, considering 9-1-1 because
an ambulance would pick him up instead.
I could sleep, then make it to work by 8:45.
He's not standing by the front door
when I look down the staircase, already dressed,
wearing what I wore out the night before.
I smell of cigarette smoke and my hair
is sticking up, like I participated in a one-night
stand. It's been years since I've gone home
with a stranger; it's been never that I drove
my father to a hospital in the middle of the night.
I brush my teeth. He's downstairs in the bathroom.
I can hear water running. I think of times I've held
an ear against another person's chest, that muffled
sound of pumping, blood moving, like the house
was alive. I put shoes on and met him in the living
room. He looks stiff from anxiety tightening him
like a malfunctioning cyborg, like bionic men
were a bad idea. I shut the lights. He turns off
the television. We walk to my car in the cold.

KELLEY
COLLIN

i put on my armor

Collin Kelley is the author of the novels *Conquering Venus* and the forthcoming *Remain in Light*, both from Vanilla Heart Publishing. His chapbook *Slow To Burn*, originally published in 2006 by MetroMania Press, was selected for the Seven Kitchens Press ReBound Series and will be re-issued in July 2011. He is also the author of the chapbook *After the Poison* (Finishing Line Press) and the self-published collection *Better To Travel*, which was nominated for the 2003 Georgia Author of the Year Award and a Lambda Literary Award. He is a multiple Pushcart Prize nominee and a recipient of the 2007 Georgia Author of the Year/Taran Memorial Award from the Georgia Writers Association at Kennesaw State University for his work as co-editor of the *Java Monkey Speaks Anthology* series from Poetry Atlanta Press. His poetry, essays, and interviews have appeared in magazines, journals, and anthologies around the world, including *Atlanta Review, Chattahoochee Review, Terminus, New Delta Review, Chiron Review* ("Garland"), *Motel 58* ("Night 65"), *Blue Fifth Review* ("Paris, Texas"), *Ecotone, MiPOesias, Tears in the Fence,* Poetz.com ("Parallel Lines"), *Contemporary American Voices* ("20th Century Boy"), and many more.

www.collinkelley.com

PHYSICAL EDUCATION
for David

I push my ass back against him,
feel his hand go slack at my throat,
subtle shifting of power as he grows
hard against my tighty-whiteys,
settling into unexplored crack,
we find empty locker room rhythm.

Before the coach returns,
he pinballs off the benches, struggles
into his too-tight Jordache jeans
and cable knit sweater, wet head
oozing through boxers, a bead
of sweat dangling off his nose.

I stand there watching, pious
in my t-shirt and Fruit of the Looms,
flaccid and un-aroused, lording
over his secret desires coaxed out
from behind year-old bully screen
and titty-twister fingers.

In PE he will never look at me again,
too busy hiding his sudden boner
from the other boys who jeer,
call him faggot, and I could save him
with one limp wrist, but this is junior high
and the smell of blood is in the air.

FIRST BLACKMAIL

I picked the movie *Absence of Malice*,
liked the way the title rolled off my tongue,
no spite in my heart in 1981.
I dragged poor goodie-two-shoes Tommy along,
my fill-in friend after Bruce turned to girls,
and we were bored and lost in the plot in 10 minutes,
even perky Sally Field couldn't keep our attention.

We played video games in the lobby,
until two girls caught Tommy's eye,
he turned on his Boy Scout charm,
like he was going for another badge,
seduced them with his *Missile Command* skills.
They giggled and gawked, ran in and out
of the theater, played hide and seek
until ushers shooed and shushed.

Tommy, dying to transcend upbringing,
hair on his chest at 13, wanted to finger fuck them,
one on each arm, a miniature playboy.
When he suggested getting naked in the bathroom,
the girls turned red and fled leaving Tommy
to rub his tented shorts, and I offered myself as substitute.

That's when Tommy got righteous, his lost religion
back with a vengeance, stronger than the need to lose cherry,
said he'd tell his mommy I was a pervert,
that I'd be banned from his basement and *Star Wars* toys.
I chanted "finger fuck, finger fuck, finger fuck"
as I unzipped him in the echoing stall, first blackmail
bouncing off the porcelain.

We rode home in silence in his parents' station wagon,
Tommy wanting to tell, rat out the ungodly,
his mouth opening and closing with silent confession,
while I hummed along to Linda Ronstadt's *Hurt So Bad*
on the radio, my lips testing new vocabulary,
the way the words absence of malice rolled off my tongue.

PARIS, TEXAS

Down the line loud and clear
snatching your voice out of Texas sky
the arid distance between us

feels complete and final
now that I know where you are
can pinpoint you on maps

or the fractured lines of my palm
fortune telling our next future
the one where we never meet again.

GARLAND

for John Gilgun

I indulge my homosexuality,
cash in a ticket for a night with Garland
on PBS singing *The Man That Got Away*.
I covet that tight navy suit, that poise.
Maybe it's true: we all want to be her.

I loved Judy when I was a child.
Maybe it's required, inbred, the deal she made
in the afterlife to keep her properly worshipped.
I got tapped young, handed my membership card,
pushed down the yellow brick road toward boys
hiding behind curtains, teasing me
with their secret things.

What I really want to know is how it feels
to sing that way, to be able to open my mouth
and have that beautiful roar issue forth, to plant
my feet and push the music out of my lungs
like some celestial dam breaking open.
To throw my head back and surrender to sounds
I make, instead of singing along with the radio.

Give me one long Cukor take, birth my secret star.
Let me slink through those slicked-backed boys
and their horns. I want to be the one-man man,
undone by my own foolishness.
I'll take her mantle, be the one who falls in love
with the no-goods, the ne'er do wells, the fags,
if I can have a voice that staggers them all
into silence and then into my open arms.

NIGHT 65

for Michael

White on black, letters and numbers
glitter and reflect off headlights,
south into Texas night,
toward San Antonio, where big sky
begins and mercury bubbles.
I am on my way to you,
we haven't met,
but you will appear like a cipher,
wearing a communist t-shirt,
carrying a bag inscribed "sexual confusion"
where I spout poetry to uninterested
youth, but not you—ageless and still—
your delicate handshake accelerating
my pulse, tugging at gravity.
You'll find ten dollars and buy my book,
act like you're meeting someone
of consequence, show up the next night
for more, tell me you're a Virgo,
our births one day apart,
then I'll never see you again.
All along the highway, the signs
Speed Limit
    75
    Night
    65
as if reduced momentum, ten clicks,
could ever save us in a crash,
spare me from racing into impossible walls.
When I leave three days later,
I will press harder, breaking the law,
speedometer topping 80.

MIDNIGHT IN A PERFECT WORLD
Russell Square, London

Standing in line at Tesco
clutching milk and batteries
my American life drops away
I blend, become unrecognizable
even to my reflection staring back
in the frozen foods door
my needled skin like sleeping limbs
as if this perfect day is a dream
from which I never want to wake.

PARALLEL LINES

My mother's mother, the one I called Moom Moom so often as a baby that it became her nickname, dances around her kitchen to Blondie singing *Heart of Glass* on the radio. It's 1979 and Debbie and the boys have sold out to disco, but the mainstream doesn't care. Dancers scream whenever the DJ spins it at the clubs, that's what my grandmother says as she teaches me The Hustle on cracked linoleum, her new husband claps along, can't take his eyes off her. Moom Moom is re-married to a trucker, divorced my one-handed, alcoholic grandfather as soon as the nest emptied, tired of the gun in her face, waking up marinated in his drunken piss. She likes long hauls, seeing the world, while my mother turns bitter and adulterous, no sizzle in the bacon my father brings home. I stay up all night to watch Blondie on the Midnight Special, learn Debbie's shawl dance with a ripped bed sheet, purloined heels, face smeared with lipstick, mother's whereabouts unknown.

JUNK

Your family
becomes completely happy with your breasts
a great opportunity to give real pleasure
feel like you're 20 again
nothing feels as good as personal pussy

Feel young, energetic and revitalized
quality medications can be cheap
it's time to enlarge your penis
live life to the fullest

You can increase the time of your sexual acts
gigantic, heavyweight, king-sized
your new cock is waiting for you
most intimate problems can be solved

Start a new life of success and happiness

20TH CENTURY BOY

The night I screamed you out of my life
for good, I fed your confettied photo
to swirling toilet, a ticker tape parade
and dead fish burial rolled into one.

Later I found the box, a jiffy popped
trove of forgotten snapshots, you
bursting in full color from every slick
surface, sulky, smirky, your mouth
issuing smoke, cigarette blurred
in your expressive hands.

If I hold them just right, I can make
a flip book of that last day,
bring you back to animated life,
the shots where you're walking away
snapping through my fingers,
your back retreating in increments,
and if I flip the other way,
you coming back.

KATE BUSH APPEARS ON NIGHT FLIGHT, 1981

Midnight in the forbidden living room,
past my parents' bedroom, closing doors quietly
behind me, unknowingly opening a path
from which I will never veer, even later
when I become older, succumb to any zeitgeist.

I turn on the TV and she somersaults
across the screen, startling the rolling vertical hold
into stillness, her siren voice makes me fumble
in the dark for volume control, I put my hand
against the screen, feel the static in my fingertips,
a transference of energy in 1981 that delineates
past and present, a woman who calls herself Cathy,
wants to come in through the window.

But she wasn't coming through, I was going in,
my link to her a series of hot boxes where she
would appear without warning over decades
like the Virgin, her songs a catechism, her name
a prayer I chanted at the backs of retreating lovers,
divorcing parents and death, and even in her absence,
the music never faltered like I did,
songs willing pills back into bottles

Twenty-seven years ago I put on my armor,
never had a ring put on my finger, blew kisses
across the ocean, for inspiration and strength,
for God to keep her even when he wasn't keeping me,
and even now, when I am driving or dancing,
walking in Los Angeles or London, the song remains
the same, her name an utterance: *Kate, Kate, Kate.*

PETERSON
EVAN J.

die young, stay pretty

Evan J. Peterson is a hagioscientist living in Seattle. His first manuscript, entirely narrated by Frankenstein's monster, is currently making the rounds with publishers. Recent or forthcoming work and reviews may be found in *Court Green*, *Lo-Ball*, *Ganymede Unfinished*, epoetryreview.com, and TheRumpus.net.

poemocracy.blogspot.com

LONG LIVE DEATH

Death is dead. You've seen to that, dear father,
enemy. Now you have no throat and yet
you try in vain to scream. I've kept you gelid
long enough, preserved within your brew.
Your boy inherits what you've left: the journals,
charts, and clues. It took me years to find it all,
your formulae for life. Now I've not seen
this look on you since I tore down your wife.

I've borne you back from Arctic cold.
You died there on the waves.
My joy, to watch your eyes grow wide—
doubtless, you're the slave.
Know this: I've brought you back to life
to choke you back to grave.

TERATONORMATIVITY

"You can get used to anything,"
            say authorities on pain.

Approaches to suffering:
                      Stockholm syndrome
                      Ecstatic fasting
                      A gash to watch it heal

or something more aesthetic:
pecked to death by peacocks, say,
            or tattooed into shock.

Embrace it: *terato-*, monster

            Bodies, modified. Split tongues,
                      lip plugs,
horns screwed into the skull.

Aren't we each monstrous to another?
                      -normativity: enforcement of a standard

            A pretty system of ugly bodies.
Girls with hooves, boys with flippers.
                      Every other tooth a fang or tusk.

To horrify and be appalled
            by every body you meet,
to lose your bladder
            in the stares of every stranger
                      on the subway.

Creatures, stalking.
The dead, walking,
unless of course
            they've lost their legs.

THE BOOK OF TERATOGENESIS

In the beginning there were insects with human faces.
Eggs hatched and snakes flew out on wasp wings.

All the cobbled beasts—Behemoth and Leviathan,
chimaera and cockatrice, dragon and sphinx—

gathered to praise chaos. They caressed one another,
kissing the joints where spider legs fused

to crocodile bodies, where the minotaur's head
bled into man. Soon, humans interbred with angels,

a race of Cain. Each one a marvel of miscegenation,
and each a warning: "Don't cross the bloodline."

Thus the Deluge. Here again, I stand like Goliath,
tempting the flood, huffing the morning breath

of mortal gods. Who can block this juggernaut?
Only God can judge me, but God, so they say,

is dead. Dead and lucky, for I am trained
in the art of aggressive resurrection.

THE CINEMA OF CRUELTY

an interview for two voices issuing from a single mouth

Monsieur Monster, please explain the Cinema of Cruelty.

A design to murder magic. A stately pleasure dome defiled. The poetry of meat.

I see. What might the audience expect to find there?

Stroboscopic surgeries. Footlights exploding, freezing actors frame by frame. Scarab beetles smashed against the screen. A shadow cast to mime the film.

Does the Cinema have a mission statement?

The inside of the body is but the outside captured. Distinctions being a marble game for hydrocephalic children. Cruelty being the copper drainage tube driven into the moron's skull. Audience participation being the only entry fee.

Is that then the goal of the Cinema, to relieve pressure?

All enjoy the smell of their own make. Each checks the pot to see what he's created. Your own filth is never quite as profane as another's.

Monsieur Monster, you speak in spongy riddles.

Of course not. Nothing is as ugly as the teeth, shredding expensive meals, mashing them down to a monochromatic lump to be squeezed lower, chamber by chamber.

I'm not sure I understand.

Prostitutes, for instance, are the avant garde in the culture war. The highest public servants of the metropolis. Abominable, how underpaid they remain. The men as hot divining rods before which aristocrats kneel and learn nothing. The women as cakes with files baked inside.

Escape, then? From what prison?

Donate your remains to art.

What?

What?

with apologies to Antonin Artaud

INTERMISSION

Allow a pause. A little calliope and a trip to the lobby.
Everyone up for a stretch, a piss, then unwashed hands
pointing at nonpareils, gummies behind the glass.
By now your eyes must be silvered over by the screen.
Rest them. You've no idea how easily they damage.
Of my own, one is blind. It can't know its own poison
green in a mirror. The other lolls as blue as asphyxia,
that necessary. But enough about me—some popcorn,

please. I like the half-burst kernels best—
hard enough to break a tooth, and tonight I did.
The thrill of surprise: chomp, chomp, shatter.
One hundred and some odd years, and I've never
lost a single molar. It's nothing, I suppose. Now,
the lights dim. Back to the show. Lift the scrim.

GODS AND MONSTERS

after The Bride of Frankenstein, *directed 1935 by James Whale*

How to sort out a sequel: monsters are difficult to kill. Hair and makeup

by burning windmill. Trailer: *The Monster Speaks!* Some revelation. Shuffle

in new characters—the queer old sorcerer, growing imps [a tarot stack in

miniature: Hierophant, Devil, Empress] like fungus from his own gray

spore. A blind man of the forest, friendship foiled again. Damn it. Ever

seen a dead man drunk? Crying? Check out the bride, Mary Shelley back

from the prologue for more, Elsa Lancaster in a fright wig to end all fright,

her gilded jaw the golden ratio of stitches. Even the laboratory is, herself,

a character, womb of stone, a mother electric. An unexpected ending:

the monster has the last word and an heroic death. And don't

you owe him that?

THE WATERMARK

after Frankenstein, *directed 1910 by J. Searle Dawley for Edison Studios*

Even in the credits, my title is handled in quotes, "the Monster." It makes
me seem ironic, arbitrary, like the watermark on each frame of film. Their
seal is on me, and I'm passed like a strumpet from one scientist to another
(doctor, director). One frays my cells as the other scratches my print. Am I
so cruel? They prod, hand in rubber gloved hand, putting the sepia into
me, watching through a keyhole as I cook. And doesn't "incarnation" even
sound painful? Imagine it—flayed in reverse, muscles struggling to hook
the bones, the pulp weaving into locks of rigid viscera. After the operation,
my face is so swollen that it hurts to cry. How do they get those mirror
shots without ever showing a camera? Film exposes everything; it reveals
nothing. A comforting distance between creature and camera,
between the screen and you, dear viewer.

EVERY NOW AND THEN I FALL APART

Last night I lost my nose. The mice
                              made off with it, proving me
                    little more than a bag of protein,

a sack of feed. Each morning I'm a heap,
                    wondering what scrap has rolled away.

What is disintegration but the breaking
                              of a chorus,
                    firing the weakest singers?
                    I don't need ten fingers.

This is how I end up in the bath
                                        days at a time.

I leak until the water congeals
                    primordial soup, prima materia,
fermenting new life.

              If I stayed still
                    for billions of years, would my bacteria
                              breed into starfish,

          manta rays, and salamanders? Into pterodactyls,
thunderbirds, and mammoths? Into
                                        men?

They would map me, prove I'm not flat.
Soon, they'd make new monsters, to wonder
                    as I do,   *Who is the ubermonster,*
              the ur-wretch on whom I grow
                    and kill and shit and fail

                    to die?

My clockwork will finally wind down. Perhaps I'll fade
                    like an image on exposed film,
and the flies will tidy up the mess.

My most hopeful member has detached,

                                                        now bobbing on the surface
                          of the bath.
             Poor scrimshaw banana,
                   scored,
                      sweet with rot.
Just another root in the soup.

DIE YOUNG, STAY PRETTY

I was a teenage Frankenstein, thighs
like bolted iron, my face and shoulders
> *Today my breast came off.*

pockmarked by sebum and the stitch,
my back like a toad's, bubbling, giving birth.
> *It slid like a slug down my belly*

Perpetual adolescent, I snapped my ankles
tripping on my own platform boots.
> *and with a magnificent suck,*

My heart was like some punk band's logo
safety-pinned against my chest,
> *it flopped onto the ground.*

half-out, exposed to air, anchored
to one nipple by a purple bulldog clip.
> *I became a man today.*

A FLY ON THE LENS

after The Fly, *directed 1986 by David Cronenberg*

I began very neatly   [the camera loves me]   but then assimilation, fusion

with the exoskeletal   zoo If film is made of silver, what is   video?

Rust?   A doctor turning baboons inside out They always turn experiments

on themselves Cue swollen   violins, followed by spectacular   wreckage

A zig   zag of warring DNA, splice of two films   Skin is grafted to chiton

[*the camera loves me*]   Proteins unzip, helixes rip apart   The insect falls

in love with his own deformity Pregnant with sutures A vat of   thread

Nibbling at this silver   stump of evolution   Test audiences needed more

convincing   [*Nude scene*] [*That'll put asses in chairs*]   [*I am made of rust*]

Zoom in tightly [*the camera loved me*]   I began very neatly

RIEL
STEVEN

a hint of god's fingers

Steven Riel is the author of three chapbooks of poems, the most recent being *Postcard from P-town*, which was runner-up for the inaugural Robin Becker Chapbook Prize and was published by Seven Kitchens Press in 2009. He received an MFA in Poetry from New England College in 2008. From 1987 to 1995, he served as poetry editor of *RFD: A Country Journal for Gay Men Everywhere*. His work has been published in anthologies and in numerous periodicals, including *The Minnesota Review*, *The Antigonish Review*, *Christopher Street*, and *Mouth of the Dragon*. He currently works as a librarian at Harvard University and teaches master's-level students of poetry at Antioch University Midwest.

www.stevenriel.com

LOST SOUL

i.

Where men park for hours in the dark,
waiting for yet another sedan
to sidle up. One pickup
departs. The whole lot
erupts in ignitions,
three-point turns for coveted spots...
                              then feigns idling
(a flock of crows with the sound turned off,
rearranging shiny wings
after the never-ending
squabble for roosts).

Rear- & side-view glances.
Fistfuls of spit.
Pubis pistons thrust steering-wheel high.
Slow-motion strolls along the lips
of lowered windows. Pilgrims, looking for.

Two white faces emerge from one night.
"You look like a lost soul," says one.
"And why are you here, Mr. High-&-Mighty?"
thinks the other, retreating from symmetrical
oil-rings reflecting off asphalt.

ii.

Mission church's white stucco defies desert,
but the side-chapel's cluttered with burned-out votives,
charred match-heads snuffed in buckets of sand.
High-&-Mighty kneels down.
In this emergency room: whispers, if at all.
Grammar-school photos,
propped against Our Lady's plaster feet.
A still-life of letters, handwritten pleas
dodging intercession's triage
into Dear Heavenly Father's inbox.
Canes, crutches, artificial legs
lean, witnesses against the railing.

In the wide surrounding valley,
saguaros spread slick mauve blossoms.

Tile cools the sanctuary,
makes midday bearable. Half an hour
in the front pew, his thumbs crossed
like altar boys', High-&-Mighty stares
at the mural's zinc-flecked blues,
crucifixion depicted near the river
where conquistador corralled Pima Alta.
On edge in this peaceful gloom,
High-&-Mighty wants to sift out
what once shone. A squat woman
in flip-flops glides out of nowhere,
folds inside his palm a white rosary,
its beads like baby teeth,
its mass-produced coil
a question he'll zip
within black recesses of his carry-on.

HELLO DOLLY

painting by Steve Walker, acrylic on canvas

Two gay G.I. Joes in Speedos
shake hands in midair, small-scale
trapeze artists with identical abs,
placed in each other's space
by two colossal hands—one tanned, one fair—
the bulk of the life-sized
men's bodies kept offstage.

"Gay" because brunet Joe unabashedly
assesses the blond's crotch
while the less worldly one
scans the eyes of his new acquaintance
for an answer that might make him
cry.

Something bestows
light behind the blond.
Though his deltoids bulge just as prodigiously,
his suit gleams diaper-white.
He sits hammocked half-way back
within the uplifted
palm of the paler statuesque hand,
offered up as sacrifice or prize.

There's a hint of God's fingers
letting Adam's go—of a firmament
beyond this blackish-blue backdrop.

The brunet, thrust from shadow,
suspended upright as if standing,
his right thigh spread wide,
gets pushed forward like a decoy
or specimen or tool ready at hand,
looks primed for all that follows
when doll skin meets.

WEEDS OF WOE

At thirteen, I wanted the whole
lot of 'em knocked off.
A fatal crash would do:
four dodos with one stone.
They wouldn't know what hit 'em.
The sympathy cards this orphan would amass!
I'd promenade down St. Paul's center aisle
tragic as Jackie K.
How could school shrinks guess
this sissy would manage just fine?
They hadn't a clue I could cook
& had scrumptious curtains
circled in the Sears catalog—
deep-violet faux-velvet drapes
framing puffy lavender sheers.
Kraft macaroni-and-cheese would frequent my menu
with a smidge of sweet pickle mix on the side—
I'd run my tongue over the bumpy
cauliflower, bite through
soft pearl onions.
Tailored in black, I'd swoop about,
trap beneath my rake each leaf that dared to flit
past pinions of my imported Inverness cape
(I'd scurry home from junior high
for Barnabas Collins rebroadcasts,
fearing & praying he'd slip into my
bedroom at dusk, make me blood-slave).

Maybe I'd snap up one of those rotting
three-story Victorians I'd coveted.
Then, I'd have my own turret,
cupola, balcony, widow's
walk—stages to pace nights away,
lofting a candle, suppressing a smile.
I'd invite neighbors to gossip
about my rambling nimbus—
I wouldn't host a tour of the Garden Club,
but I wouldn't pull my shades, either,
as I ogled undershorts in catalogs

& heaved prodigious sighs.
Miss Havisham would have nothing on me.

——

But when scythe *did* rend
one of us dodos,
sever: bloody feathers.
After: strewn twigs
of a ground bird's pilfered nest. Forever:
never never Camp.

ALL SET

Darling, I've rearranged the plates
since you arrived. Do you think shaken
cocktails loosen tongues at random,
evening undrapes before being ironed
then re-hooked? I hold the burning iron.
It glides as I please. *Voulez-vous
promenez? Avec quelque chose à*—
guess who's going to dine
on your left? Yes, of course he left
his card. Smell: cologne. Feel:
creamy stock. I knew you'd have wanted
warning, wouldn't have elected ambush,
wouldn't have chosen blush. Hush.
We mustn't give away our hands.
Hearts? Hold them close
long past dessert, when they'll trip up
trump. Pattern? A pinkish-blue
by Fabergé. To die for. Wait and see.
Fold? We've only just begun
to bid. Powder room? Why bother?
There's nothing else to do.

SIGHTED DURING A WHALE WATCH

To commune with late afternoon's muted light,
to swathe myself in swirls of solitude,
I turn from those aiming sleek cell phones,
zooming Nikons in on hennaed roots.
My grip loose around portside railing,
I'm a cave open toward uncluttered
ocean.

August breeze and lukewarm spray
soothe even my readily goose-bumped flesh.
The wounded creature I've become
unclenches, sways with the hull's lullaby.
With windbreaker unzipped, I stand becalmed,
adrift.

When massed clouds divide, sunlight sprints
across napping waves, spreads across my brow,
as if laying outstretched palms
tender against my temples.
For sixteen years, I never imagined,
couldn't have expected nor prepared for
my dead brother's palpable
presence.

Unbidden, warm salt streams
down creek-bed creases in my face
as if a switch were thrown
offstage

and all glistens within one membrane:
brine-tangy air, trembling sea, fireball low in the firmament
transmitting this gentle sheet of sheen—
something free of his personality.
It feels

open, angelic. Even after cumulous
bulges back across the blazing gap,
I linger over the vast, now-pearly bay,
not wanting to step away from that near
caress.

Someone else could call it an ordinary excursion—
just more whales than usual bless us with tail-flips
as they herd krill toward one spot.
We applaud and tip the salty captain.
And yes, a similar shaft of light, overdone in oils
and framed in some knickknack shop, can be bought,
or witnessed when Yahweh's voice booms
in an Old Testament film staring Heston,
but

when that wedge of light arrowed across,
what my skin and eyes at once recognized
marks these years without: before and after.
I don't know whether he'll visit
again.

ROBERT GOULET IS DEAD!

With your demise, one
sure-fire aphrodisiac flickers

but never goes out.
Five years old, hips
jammed against the fabric front
of our cabinet-sized stereo, I slithered
to where hidden speakers buzzed beneath
holster me   bolster me   tingle of your baritone
coxswain & oarsman
deep & firm & strong.

"If ever I should leave you,"
even down the hall, I'd tent, hard-
wired eardrum to hardwired taint.

If I place this disc just so,
we'll move together again:
Morocco me   embargo me
beverage & gargle me
roll me up & cabbage me
stallion as I lather you

Have me on a platter, please,
if you fancy food. Just
thrust all through a low note.
I wait in marinade.
You sound the sure vibrato.
You growl the deep-down way. Your dying
father made you vow to use the gift Dieu gave.
Merci, Père, for handing 'Tit-Gars the key
that turns the bolt in me:
wire me   high note   *fire me*
Conduit of dream.
I'm a socket hoping to be plugged;
a glance waiting to be met;
weak-kneed; obvious; a dizzy, cheap drunk;
shish-kabob, meatballs
laid out on a buffet
ladle me   cradle me
If ever you should leave her

reflect & connect
me   me   me
look up my number
on any heavenly wall.

KLEIN
MICHAEL

a student of classics

Michael Klein recently published his second book of poems, *then, we were still living*, with GenPop Books. His first book, *1990*, tied with James Schulyer to win the Lambda Book Award in 1993. Recent work appears in *Bloom*, *Post Road*, and *Lambda Literary Review*. He is working on a new book of poems with the working title, *What I'm Going to Do Is...*

www.boypoet.com

HOW TO READ A POEM IN 2012

If there's enough light
you can read anything
so I don't need glasses
to see newsprints of violence
or characters in bold type running the world—to see
the newsprint of Bruce's new poems in the *American Poetry Review*.
I will want to know what Bruce has to say long after
I have listened to others who are talking more than Bruce.
His poems feel as though what he remembers and what he lives
    make a double exposure
not a frame around the sequence of living,
    or the conundrum there in the light behind the lines:
How do we live without violence in the already violent world?
    They are always
strong—Bruce's poems—like a man's hand opening.
And without the glasses, the ends of lines blur
into prose and are not about a poet named Bruce at all.
They are about what we did to this world
    and what we must do now that we've done it.

GHOST

The body is everywhere.

He knew that right at the let go.

Suspend, the room said to the wire of mind, as it instructed the body.

When he comes back, days are spent in the cities

crossing back and forth

the streets or states of regret.

I know him everyday: just there: at the edge of life:

where it feels like work. He comes back to do

something he could say was *last*.

There's Kevin, my twin brother,

one day sober, trying to light a cigarette in the wind.

The body is everything.

WASHING THE CORPSE

Spirit always wants the door.

After he was dead they washed his body.

Nick and Michael and Michael stood in Billy's hospital room
and after whatever it was stopped making the room vibrate and lighten and
become heavy again they took the washcloth or whatever it was—
something from the hospital, something rising hot
out of the silver basin—and started at his feet
and worked their way up the body that was only his body on the bed.

And Marie and Janice and Julie who had been in the room
while the spirit was directing the air had left the room
so that it was only now the men
doing the last thing that would ever be done to Billy's body.
They were making Billy new.
They were making Billy *what was over.*

DISTRICT 9

It was a metaphor
for AIDS, for Apartheid, for the other
living on the margin—to think
they only just want to get into the place
everybody lives in.

There was a time, when all revolts began, where we lived
on the margin to make the margin wider.

THE GIFT OF PROPHESY

You'll remember a trip south;

the woman you went to live with for awhile;

the woman you told cancer

when you didn't have cancer. You said

you were dying of the current dying

because you didn't know how else it could all be taken: what nobody

can say: *I am living of something.*

THE BED

Night for him is whatever that was in Hyde's
beaker to bring on Jekyll—alcohol—a student of
classics will tell you.

Or was it just
all day dropping all scenes on his heart?

There'll be intimacy,
every man says in bed.

THE SAME DREAM

Every night for months I've had a variation of the same dream.
I'm in a school. I'm the teacher.

The dream world comes and sits in a room.
We are speaking in a language that no one has heard before
but which everybody understands.
Welcome dream world.

There is a moment of a high wind blowing

and a moment of sunlight brightening more

and making the scene hard to see.

Inside the fold of sun and wind, there are more women than there are men.

Then, there is an animal – usually a four-legged animal.

At some point in the dream, somebody always comes back to life.

At some point in the dream, somebody doesn't come into the room.

FDR DRIVE

There's a sacred place on the FDR Drive
where a car can be the eye inside the East
River and the future of traffic and water
is the way upper left of what if this were a painting and I am alive in it.

You can see what will happen and what is happening
now in the same view.

But instead of mortal cars into the sky, I am thinking
of the racehorse and what *seeing* means in his life
and if this were his race he would
know that desire holds more than time which is why
someone in the human class is always on a kind of rail
to watch him.

POLITICS

They want me to talk. My voice
is back and they want me to tell them
how it really happened. In my voice, apparently,
what really happened sounds different
once it is heard, unpacked from its box of voices.
My voice makes anything I say sound like something
I just found out. And probably,
hazardly, maybe, and troubling, of all the voices in this unnerving
world, they want me to use mine, the man and the woman who
are telling me all this with their heads in the open window
this voice, the one
that is awake now and living outside of its box
tell them certainly how it is,
and who the people are, and how it really happened,
and what they're going to have to do now,
now that they've heard my voice saying
what it can never say.

AMAZABLE

Who are we without wanting

anymore what we did not know?

Knowledge isn't art.

There was fire left in the paint

when Van Gogh finished his painting

about rain and called it something else.

MORAN
MICHAEL

fallen angel

Michael Moran, who graciously donated the cover art for this issue of *Assaracus*, was born in West Springfield, Massachusetts. He studied art from 1984 to 1989 on Shelter Island, New York, under August Mosca, a noted New York artist. He attended the Art Students League in New York City from 1989 to 1990. Since then he has spent much time and private study developing his artistic talents. He paints in oils and acrylics and draws in pencil, pen and ink, and silverpoint. He is an unabashed realist, painting landscape, still life, and the figure. One of his specialties is painting icons, translating this ancient art form of the Eastern Christian churches into contemporary terms. His work has been exhibited since 1985 in galleries and museums largely in Illinois, Kentucky, New York, Pennsylvania and Texas. He has painted commissions both in the United States and abroad, and his work is in many private collections. He may be contacted by email at mmbx51@aol.com.

www.angelstudiostore.com

SUBMIT TO ASSARACUS

The mission of Sibling Rivalry Press is to develop, publish, and promote outlaw artistic talent—those projects which inspire people to read, challenge, and ponder the complexities of life in dark rooms, under blankets by cell-phone illumination, in the backseats of cars, and on spring-day park benches next to people reading Baldwin and Angelou. We encourage submissions to *Assaracus* by gay male poets of any age, regardless of background, education, or level of publication experience. For more information, visit us online.

www.siblingrivalrypress.com

Lightning Source UK Ltd.
Milton Keynes UK
UKOW051055200812

197778UK00002B/251/P